THE WINNING MINDSET WORKBOOK

By

Sugar Ray Destin, Jr.

Co-authored by Powerful World Changers

2022

The Winning Mindset

WORKBOOK

Sugar Ray Destin, Jr.
and
Powerful World Changers

First Printing: 2022

ISBN: 979-8-9868620-0-2

Ordering Information:

Special discounts are available on quantity purchases by corporations, associations, educators, and others. For details, contact the publisher at the email listed below.

U.S. trade bookstores and wholesalers:
Please contact info@businessofbooksmastermind.com.

DEDICATION

This book is dedicated to my son, Zayden, my Niecee Makhi, and all the young people chasing their dreams. Live your dreams and always soar beyond the limitations of others!

TABLE OF CONTENTS

FOREWORD

When we were asked to write the foreword for this book, we jumped at the opportunity. The topic of having a winning mindset exemplifies our son and the authors in this book. To give you some context, we have shared a little about the character of our baby boy. We know that you'll enjoy this book as much as we have watched him grow through life and become the man he is today.

Sugar Ray is very much into God. His beliefs are inspiring. As a teenager he became a bible study teacher. He started off as a toddler at a Montessori school. Later he went on to attend St. Christopher Catholic School for his kindergarten year. He was tested to get into public school at the age of 5 for his first-grade year. He read his sister's books as early as one years old. He also used to beg his sister to read to him in those early days.

He learned at a high level by paying attention to others while observing their skills. He's very meticulous about his work and passionate about helping others. He's always thought beyond his years. He does not like being around negativity. He often says, "If you can't say anything nice, then don't say it at all."

He's focused on his goals and will not let obstacles stand in his way. He thrives under pressure and carries himself with a spirit of excellence.

Carolyn J. Destin

As a parent, first of all I need to congratulate my son, Sugar Ray, for picking himself back up by his bootstraps. He took time to slowly and strategically planning his work, then working his plan. He should take a serious look in the mirror and pat himself on the back for how far he's come.

Sugar Ray has always been an overachiever. Especially when it comes to educational school programs. He was always able to overcome obstacles because once he put his mind to really learn something, he gave it his all. People think it's easy for him because they're looking from the outside in. However, we've seen the hours of frustration he endures and how hard he works to get to the point that he's risen to.

Sugar Ray Destin, Sr.

PREFACE

To each of you reading this book, we want to thank you. There are many other noteworthy books on the shelf, and you chose to add this book to your collection. We truly appreciate you for making that decision.

Inside the pages of this book, you will read some amazing stories about triumph in the face of adversity. You will be challenged to walk into a new realm of possibilities for your life. The phenomenal authors in this book come from a variety of backgrounds including entrepreneurs, speakers, mental health specialists, brand managers, professional athletes, movie producers, educators, financial planners, and world changers. Each author has shared strategies to help you live your best life and reframe your mental capacity. If you apply the tips given in this book, you will find yourself soaring to a level in your life.

This book was designed to be a complete movement that shifts the dynamic and changes lives around the globe. There is also a workbook and coaching program that compliments this book. Please be sure to grab you copy of the workbook and connect with a certified Winning Mindset Coach to take your life to the highest level possible.

We would love to hear about your future success. From the bottom of our hearts, we love you, believe in you, and are rooting for your ultimate success!

Signed with love,

The Authors of The Winning Mindset

LIST OF AUTHORS IN CHAPTER ORDER

1. Sugar Ray Destin, Jr.
2. Adrienne E. Bell
3. Channell M Dawson
4. Charles Woods
5. Chip Baker
6. Darryl W. Thomas, Jr.
7. Derrick Pearson
8. Deuce Malone
9. Ereka Howard, M.S.
10. Hoss Tabrizi
11. Kenneth Wilson
12. Kristen Davis
13. Monica Earl Washington
14. Reggie Rusk

DESTINED FOR GREATNESS!
Sugar Ray Destin, Jr.

Are you competitive?

- o Yes
- o No

What is the thing that drives you to become successful?

_____
_____
_____
_____
_____
_____
_____
_____
_____
_____

Who are the people that inspired you in your younger days?

_____
_____
_____
_____
_____
_____
_____
_____
_____
_____
_____
_____

What are some of the values they instilled in you?

_____
_____
_____
_____
_____
_____
_____
_____
_____
_____
_____
_____
_____
_____
_____

What are some of the sacrifices you've made throughout life?

_____
_____
_____
_____
_____
_____
_____
_____
_____
_____
_____
_____
_____
_____
_____
_____
_____

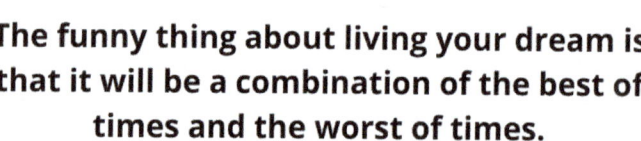

The funny thing about living your dream is that it will be a combination of the best of times and the worst of times.

Who is your competition?

_____
_____
_____
_____
_____
_____
_____
_____
_____
_____

Do you collaborate with your competitors?
- o Yes
- o No

What have you learned from your competition?

_____
_____
_____
_____
_____
_____
_____
_____
_____
_____
_____
_____
_____
_____
_____

Do you challenge yourself to learn more than others in your field?
- o Yes
- o No

What are some of the things you need to learn in your current field to advance to the next level?

_____
_____
_____
_____
_____
_____
_____
_____
_____
_____
_____
_____
_____
_____
_____
_____
_____
_____
_____
_____
_____
_____
_____

> **Through it all, the goal has always been the same ... help as many people as I can to achieve their dreams and leave a legacy for the generations coming behind me. That's what a winning mindset is to me, sticking to your principles, empowering others to succeed, and understanding that you're going to ruffle a few feathers along the way.**

Do you surround yourself with people from other ethnic and communal backgrounds?
- o Yes
- o No

Are you in an environment that celebrates or tolerates you?
- o The people in my environment celebrates my accomplishments
- o The people in my environment makes my accomplishments seem small

Are you in environments that expose you to successful people?
- o Yes
- o No

Do you still hold on to unresolved wounds from your past?
- o Yes
- o No

What organizations connected to your field are you actively participating in?

_____
_____
_____
_____
_____
_____
_____
_____
_____
_____
_____
_____
_____
_____
_____
_____
_____
_____
_____
_____
_____
_____
_____
_____
_____
_____

Have you ever had a breakthrough moment in your life?

- o Yes
- o No

Describe the breakthrough moment in your personal life:

_____
_____
_____
_____
_____
_____
_____
_____
_____
_____
_____
_____
_____
_____
_____
_____
_____
_____
_____
_____
_____
_____
_____
_____
_____
_____
_____
_____
_____
_____
_____
_____
_____

If you could make your dreams a reality, write the list of your accomplishments that will occur in the next ten years:

_____

_____

_____

_____

_____

_____

_____

_____

_____

_____

_____

_____

_____

_____

_____

_____

_____

_____

_____

_____

_____

_____

_____

_____

_____

_____

_____

_____

_____

_____

_____

_____

_____

_____

_____

_____

_____

_____

In the midst of it all, I want to remind you that you were born to win.

I challenge you to tap into your personal level of greatness and focus on being the best version of yourself possible.

Remember, on the road to your dreams, some people will love you and some will hate you.

OWN YOUR LANE AND ...
SUCCEED ANYWAY!

ABOUT THE AUTHOR:

See Lead Author's Bio in About the Author section.

THE PRICE IS THE PRICE!
Adrienne E. Bell

Have you ever had a meeting with a potential client that seemed interested in your services?

- o Yes
- o No

Did the potential client show extreme enthusiasm about working with you based on your rave reviews?

- o Yes
- o No

Place a check beside the following statements that you have heard from a prospective consumer:

- o IS THAT THE PRICE?
- o Are you running any specials?
- o Is there any way I can get a discount?
- o I was on Google and the services you are offering do not cost that much! People actually pay you that much?

> **THE PRICE IS THE PRICE! STOP allowing people to adjust the price of your products, goods, or services just because they demand it.**

It is vital to your success as an entrepreneur to develop your pricing structure based on industry-standard rates AND your receipts.

List 5-10 accomplishments/qualifications in your field of expertise:

_____

_____

_____

_____

_____

_____

_____

_____

_____

_____

_____

_____

_____

_____

_____

_____

_____

_____

_____

_____

_____

_____

_____

_____

_____

_____

_____

> **It is *your responsibility* to communicate how beneficial (valuable) you are to their project. It is up to them to see if the value (benefits) you presented to them is "worth" paying for!**

You cannot effectively create and sell your products or services until you GET CLEAR about your worth to the client and value to yourself. You first have to view pricing your products and services from the customer's point of view, NOT YOURS.

List the top 5 services you currently offer and provide a brief description of each:

1. _____

    _____

    _____

    _____

2. _____

    _____

    _____

    _____

    _____

3. _____

    _____

    _____

    _____

4. _____

    _____

    _____

    _____

5. _____

    _____

    _____

    _____

List the benefits of the first service listed above:

_____

_____

_____

_____

_____

_____

_____

_____

_____

_____

_____

List the benefits of the second service listed above:

_____

_____

_____

_____

_____

_____

_____

_____

_____

_____

_____

_____

_____

_____

List the benefits of the third service listed above:

_____
_____
_____
_____
_____
_____
_____
_____
_____
_____

List the benefits of the fourth service listed above:

_____
_____
_____
_____
_____
_____
_____
_____
_____
_____

List the benefits of the fifth service listed above:

_____

_____

_____

_____

_____

_____

_____

_____

_____

_____

_____

_____

_____

> **You have to create an incredibly sexy pricing model where they see the value you see and realize you're worth it! You do not have to make excuses for charging clients fairly for your services.**

Would YOU pay the price you are charging clients?

- o Yes
- o No

If the price is the price, make sure it is a price YOU would actually pay.

There is an epidemic in entrepreneurship where service providers are not only OVERCHARGING clients, but most are UNDERCHARGING. If you struggle knowing your value to yourself and your worth to the client, don't beat yourself up. We have all been there.

Do you know your worth to potential clients?

- o Yes
- o No

Are you valuing yourself properly?

- o Yes
- o No

Here are a few tips to a WINNING MINDSET when it comes to pricing structure:

1. The price is the price. Period. Do not allow anyone to cause you to change your price.
2. If you decide to change your price or discount your services, let it be YOUR decision. Do not be coerced into lowering your standards OR your price. If you wouldn't do it, don't do it for the client.
3. Be fair to the client as well as yourself. Whether you have 10,000 hours of experience or ten, you are valuable, and your worth is NEVER for sale.
4. The days of the "solopreneur" are over. People treat you differently when they think you are operating alone. They take their entitlement to lower prices to another level when they feel you are the only one pocketing the profit. To scale your business to a six, seven, or eight-figure business, you must build a team and a system that can be automated. You have the potential to deliver high-quality services to your clients and reach greater earning potential when you create the right system and build the right team. Having a team and an automated business model will automatically justify your pricing model.
5. Price your goods and services to turn a profit. Make sure you price your services where you net between 40-50% of your gross revenue. That is an aggressive number, but it is a good goal to reach for as you are creating or revamping your pricing structure. If you can't keep it between 40-50, do your best not to go below 20%.
6. Be humble but confident when establishing your prices. Don't allow fear of losing the sale to keep you from being paid fairly. Don't allow yourself to compare your pricing structure to another service provider. Remember, they may have skills, expertise, or experience that you may not have. On the contrary, you may need to increase your price if you have training or experience that someone else may not have.
7. The more you grow as a service provider, the more you should charge. With the cost of inflation, gas prices, and the cost of goods, you must find out how much you are spending on supplies to ensure you are making a profit.

Answer the following questions:

How much is your hour worth?

_____

Who is my ideal client and why?

_____

_____

_____

_____

_____

_____

_____

What are my deal-breakers when securing a client?

_____

_____

_____

_____

Where can I find my ideal client?

_____

_____

_____

Why am I struggling with properly pricing my products and services? Fear? Shame? Value? Worth?

_____

_____

_____

_____

_____

_____

_____

_____

Describe the clientele you are attracting?

_____

_____

_____

_____

Are you attracting people with a poverty mindset?

- o Yes
- o No

Are you attracting people who look for discounts and rebates versus value and quality?

- o Yes
- o No

Do you do to vendors what you don't want clients to do to you?

- o Yes
- o No

Do you ask for discounts and rebates?

- o Yes
- o No

You cannot become upset with clients when they ask for deals if you do the same thing to other service providers. You reap what you sow.

Are you having trouble with pricing? Hire a brand strategist or pricing specialist to help you create or reconfigure your pricing model. You cannot grow your business effectively until you know how to charge the right price for the service you are providing. The price is the price! Don't discount yourself and don't let anyone else do it either!

ABOUT THE AUTHOR:

Social Media:

IG @therealadriennebell

FB @therealadriennebell

LinkedIn: @adrienneebell

Email therealadriennebell@gmail.com

Adrienne E. Bell is a 22x Amazon Bestselling Publisher, Executive Producer of the soul-stirring Amazon Prime movie, "When the Soul Cries: Trauma. Tears. Triumph." and Executive Brand Management Expert.

"My superpower is to energize, empower, and encourage executives, authors, coaches, speakers, and thought leaders to be legendary in business, love, and relationships. Let's Work!"

SIGNATURE TALKS

1. **The Price Is The Price!** - *"The price is the price, but for some of us, the price is NOT RIGHT!"*
2. **The Wifeabilty Framework** - *"If you don't friend well, you won't wife well."*
3. **Loyalty Is Optional** - *"Don't expect loyalty from others when you aren't loyal to yourself."*

SERVICES OFFERED

- *Brand Development*
- *Brand Management*
- *Project Management*
- *Non-Profit Development*
- *Revenue Planning*
- *Event Planning & Management*
- *Product Development & Launches*
- *Website Development and SEO*
- *Business Funding & More!*

A BETTER LIFE
Channell M. Dawson

> **To obtain a winning mindset, one must have the mind of Christ.**

Can you recognize the blessings God has given you?

- o Yes
- o No

List 5 things you are grateful for today:

1. _____
2. _____
3. _____
4. _____
5. _____

Do you control your daily thoughts?

When we talk about mindset, we are talking about the results of our inner thoughts made manifest in our day-to-day interactions and dealings with other human beings.

o Yes

o No

What do you do daily to control your thoughts?

_____
_____
_____
_____
_____
_____
_____
_____
_____
_____
_____
_____
_____
_____
_____

> **If we don't apply what is in us, we will never strike it rich mentally, spiritually, emotionally, or financially.**

Make a list of your top strengths and talents:

1. _____
2. _____
3. _____
4. _____
5. _____
6. _____
7. _____
8. _____
9. _____
10. _____

How are you applying your talents each day?

_____
_____
_____
_____
_____
_____
_____
_____
_____
_____

> **Winners don't focus on the fans they focus on the finish line. Winners know that when they get to the finish line of their current level that it's time to start training for their next level.**

What are the top 3 things you focus on each day?

1. _____
2. _____
3. _____

Developing a Winning Mindset

What information do you take in to improve your talents?

_____
_____
_____
_____
_____
_____
_____

Success requires sacrifice. What are you willing to sacrifice to become successful?

_____
_____
_____
_____
_____
_____

> **The truth is that we were created to win! Anything that stands in the way of our success we should be willing to lay it aside until we achieve what we desire in our heart to achieve.**

Do you have a mentor or Mindset Coach?

- o   Yes
- o   No

If not, why?

_____

_____

_____

_____

If so, in what areas have you improved?

_____

_____

_____

_____

_____

_____

_____

_____

_____

_____

_____

> **A winning mindset is focused on the connection, then communication, and finally the completion of the assignment. Once the assignment is complete the purpose and prosperity will explode and overflow into something that will bless one generation to the next.**

Who are the top 5 people in your circle?

1. _____

2. _____

3. _____

4. _____

5. _____

Do the people in your circle motivate you or pull you down?

- ○ Yes

- ○ No

Are you passing a winning mindset on to your family and those around you?

- ○ Yes

- ○ No

Remember these tips:

We were created by God in His image and His likeness and just like He is—we are perfect!

Winning is what we were created to do!

Our mind is designed to win!!!

When we set our minds on things greater than our current situations winning is our portion!!!

Nothing or no one can stop a winning mindset because it is focused on the finish line, not the audience or onlookers!!!

ABOUT THE AUTHOR:

Social Media:

IG @cdawson0425

FB @cdawson0425

LinkedIn: @channelldawson

Email cdawson0425@gmail.com

Mrs. Channell Maiden Dawson, serves as an employee of the federal government for sixteen years, including positions in leadership. She enjoys using these leadership skills to develop other leaders.

Dawson draws inspiration from her husband of 18 years, 15-year-old daughter, and her three-year-old boy/girl twins. In Mrs. Dawson's free time, activities include motivational speaking, encouraging leaders to be greater leaders, working with underprivileged individuals with avenues to become privileged in their endeavors, and undereducated individuals to seek means of higher education for career and life advancement.

Dawson earned an Associate's Degree in Christian Counseling along with 19 years of experience in marriage, parenting, and career counseling. She holds multiple life coaching certifications including master life coach, life purpose coach, happiness life coach, mindset coach, cognitive behavior coach, goal success coach, and professional life coach.

Channell M. Dawson serves as the President of Lifestyle Restoration Group (LRG) a 501c3 non-profit organization that provides an opportunity for growth and development in whatever portion of our client's life that seems to be unfruitful or unproductive whether is a failing marriage, broken relationship, or lack of motivation in you career path we can help get our clients to get back on the road to success.

At the end of every encounter with individuals or family units, her mission is to assist them with the pursuit of living a blessed life so everyone can see them live their best lives and prove the doubters wrong.

THINK GREAT! DO GREAT! BE GREAT!

Charles Woods

> Life is about choices, making the best choice for your well-being, and the well-being of those in your presence. Life is not always good but there are opportunities every day, every hour, every minute, every second to change your outcomes, but only if that is your desire.

What are you thankful for in your life currently?

_____

_____

_____

_____

_____

_____

_____

_____

Are you happy or envious of other people's success?

o Yes

o No

Have you created a plan for your life?

- o Yes
- o No

What are your top 3 short term (next 3-5 years) goals?

1. _____
   _____
2. _____
   _____
3. _____
   _____

What is your plan to make your first goal a reality?

_____
_____
_____
_____
_____

What is your plan to make your second goal a reality?

_____
_____
_____
_____
_____

What is your plan to make your third goal a reality?

_____
_____
_____
_____
_____

The key is to develop a plan that is focused on having a better life and implementing that plan. You control your future and everything in it.

What is your long-term (10-20 years) life goal?

_____
_____
_____
_____
_____

What is your plan to make your long-term goal a reality?

_____
_____
_____
_____
_____
_____
_____
_____
_____
_____
_____
_____
_____
_____

Trait: Grateful

- **For every day you get to open your eyes and have an opportunity to be better**
- **For the individuals that came before you and made it possible for you to have these opportunities**
- **For everyone that took the time to support you on your journey**

What are the 5 things you are most grateful for?

1. _____
2. _____
3. _____
4. _____
5. _____

Who are the people that helped open doors or paved the road to your success?

1. _____
2. _____
3. _____
4. _____
5. _____
6. _____
7. _____

Who are your top supporters?

1. _____
2. _____
3. _____
4. _____
5. _____
6. _____
7. _____

> **There will always be opportunities that will present themselves. Acceptance of those opportunities is where the decision needs to be made. Understand that these opportunities may not come easy.**

Do you know how to recognize the opportunities in front of you?

- o   Yes
- o   No

What are some opportunities that you can take advantage of immediately to help you on your journey?

_____
_____
_____
_____
_____
_____
_____
_____
_____
_____
_____
_____
_____
_____
_____
_____
_____

Are you persistent enough to overcome the obstacles that come with these opportunities?

- o   Yes
- o   No

Have you ever allowed life's trials to stop you from pursuing your goals?

- o   Yes
- o   No

What could you have done differently when you faced the situation?

_____

_____

_____

_____

_____

_____

_____

_____

_____

_____

What are some obstacles you foresee in pursuit of your current goals?

1. _____
2. _____
3. _____
4. _____
5. _____

What steps will you take if faced with the first obstacle listed?

_____

_____

_____

_____

_____

What steps will you take if faced with the second obstacle listed?

_____

_____

_____

_____

_____

What steps will you take if faced with the third obstacle listed?

_____

_____

_____

_____

_____

What steps will you take if faced with the fourth obstacle listed?

_____

_____

_____

_____

_____

What steps will you take if faced with the fifth obstacle listed?

_____

_____

_____

_____

_____

Trait: Energy

- **Your energy controls your productivity**
- **Your energy will determine your outcomes**
- **Positive energy and thoughts will drive your success and keep you motivated throughout the process**

Energy is important and everyone has the choice of which type of energy will be allowed in and what type of energy will be put out. Life is so much easier when energy is focused in a positive direction.

Do you give off good energy daily?

- o   Yes
- o   No

What do you do daily to get your energy right?

_____

_____

_____

_____

_____

_____

_____

_____

_____

_____

_____

_____

_____

_____

Trait: Accountable

- **There is no individual that can hold you more accountable than yourself. Take on the challenge and monitor yourself**
- **Be willing to allow someone to take on the responsibility of being your accountability partner when needed**

Do you take accountability for your own success?

- o   Yes
- o   No

Survey the 5 people closest to you and ask them what they think about your work ethic:

1. _____
_____
_____

2. _____
_____
_____

3. _____
_____
_____

4. _____
_____
_____

5. _____
_____
_____

Do you have an accountability partner or group?

- o   Yes
- o   No

Trait: Trust

- **Make sure you are exhibiting characteristics and actions that will build a foundation of trust. Be willing and execute the ability to believe and rely on others**
- **Always be firm but fair. Lead with a kind heart and care for others, but the expectations are the expectations.**

Do you see yourself as a leader?

- o Yes

- o No

Have you established a team to help you achieve your goals?

- o Yes

- o No

List the people on your success team:

1. _____
2. _____
3. _____
4. _____
5. _____

Do you value the members of your team?

- o Yes

- o No

Does your team trust you?

- o Yes

- o No

1. **Think GREAT** (Think of your needs personally and/or professionally and how these traits will support you on your journey of growth.)

2. **Do GREAT** (Develop a plan that consists of these traits and is focused on your growth. You may have already established one or more of the traits but remember there is always room to grow.)

3. **Be GREAT** (This is a lifetime journey that is filled with reflection and adjustments. Continue to put in the work and the outcomes will be GREAT.)

ABOUT THE AUTHOR:

Social Media:

IG @charleswoodsww

FB @charleswoodsww

LinkedIn: @charleswoodsww

Email ullgrad1911@hotmail.com

Charles has nineteen years in public education, nine years as a classroom teacher and football coach, six years as a head boys track coach, five years as an assistant principal and this year makes his fifth year as a building principal.

Charles has a M.S. in Engineering and Technology Management and a B.S. in Industrial Technology from the University of Louisiana at Lafayette. He is a four time best selling author for his collaborative work in Black Men Love and The Impact Of Influence Volume 1, 2 and 4. Charles takes pride in being a Positive Mindset and Motivational Mentor, Coach and Speaker. He is married to his beautiful wife Celena Woods and has two daughters Courtney and Chelsea Greer.

His certifications include:

- EC-12 Superintendent Certification
- EC-12 Principal Certification
- EC-12 Special Education Certification
- Rice University Leadership Partner's Executive Education Academy
- Non Crisis Intervention Trainer

"There is no other profession that gives me the opportunity to impact lives like public education. I did not choose this path; this path chose me. I will continue to be a servant leader to those in my care and for those that choose to work with me. I am forever grateful for this opportunity to make a difference in the lives of our young scholars."

"Don't be a product of your environment, make your environment be a product of the positive you!!!"

MINDSET IS DEVELOPED BY UNDERSTANDING LIMITS, POSSIBILITIES AND OPPORTUNITIES

Chip Baker

> **A winning mindset, like anything, must be developed. In order to win on a consistent basis, one must have a mindset that continues to grow. A person that understands that there are no limits to what they can achieve, will soar to high heights.**

"If you limit yourself, you limit yourself."

-Chip Baker

Do you place limits on yourself?

- o Yes
- o No

Do you allow others to place limits on you?

- o Yes
- o No

Do you take time daily to evaluate your progress?

- o Yes
- o No

Are you further ahead in pursuit of your goals now than before?

- o Yes
- o No

What are five things you need to improve on in pursuit of your goals?

1. _____
2. _____
3. _____
4. _____
5. _____

What will you do to improve on the first item listed?

_____
_____
_____
_____

What will you do to improve on the second item listed?

_____
_____
_____
_____

What will you do to improve on the third item listed?

_____
_____
_____
_____

What will you do to improve on the fourth item listed?

_____

_____

_____

_____

What will you do to improve on the fifth item listed?

_____

_____

_____

_____

Is your self-talk positive or negative?

o   Positive

o   Negative

If your self-talk is negative, explain why:

_____

_____

_____

_____

_____

List ten positive attributes about yourself:

1. _____
2. _____
3. _____
4. _____
5. _____
6. _____
7. _____
8. _____
9. _____
10. _____

"The possibilities are possible."

-Chip Baker

Do you compare your success to the success of others?

- o Yes
- o No

Do you allow the success of others to motivate you?

- o Yes
- o No

List five people that are more successful than you, currently:

1. _____
2. _____
3. _____
4. _____
5. _____

What lessons can you learn from the first person you listed?

_____
_____
_____
_____
_____

What lessons can you learn from the second person you listed?

_____

_____

_____

_____

_____

What lessons can you learn from the third person you listed?

_____

_____

_____

_____

_____

What lessons can you learn from the fourth person you listed?

_____

_____

_____

_____

_____

What lessons can you learn from the fifth person you listed?

_____

_____

_____

_____

_____

What will you implement in your own life and work ethic based on the lessons listed above?

_____

_____

_____

_____

_____

"Opportunities bring opportunities."

-Chip Baker

Are you giving your best effort when opportunities being presented to you?

o   Yes

o   No

Have you experienced additional opportunities because of previous opportunities?

o   Yes

o   No

Are you building productive relationships with others?

o   Yes

o   No

What opportunities have you experienced because of your network?

_____

_____

_____

_____

_____

_____

_____

List ten people who are not in your network that you would like to connect with for business purposes:

1. _____
2. _____
3. _____
4. _____
5. _____
6. _____
7. _____
8. _____
9. _____
10. _____

Who's in your network that can connect you with the first person you listed?

_____
_____
_____

Who's in your network that can connect you with the second person you listed?

_____
_____
_____

Who's in your network that can connect you with the third person you listed?

_____
_____
_____

Who's in your network that can connect you with the fourth person you listed?

_____
_____
_____

Who's in your network that can connect you with the fifth person you listed?

_____

_____

_____

Who's in your network that can connect you with the sixth person you listed?

_____

_____

_____

Who's in your network that can connect you with the seventh person you listed?

_____

_____

_____

Who's in your network that can connect you with the eighth person you listed?

_____

_____

_____

Who's in your network that can connect you with the ninth person you listed?

_____

_____

_____

Who's in your network that can connect you with the tenth person you listed?

_____

_____

_____

Are you willing to connect others in your network to help them succeed?

- o   Yes
- o   No

> **When we are thankful for what we are blessed to have it shows that we do not take each opportunity for granted. We show that we understand that things could be better, but they could also be much worse. We will gain more opportunities from valuing each experience.**

"Valuing adds value."

-Chip Baker

Are you grateful for the opportunities you have each day?

- o Yes
- o No

Do you place value on the opportunities you have?

- o Yes
- o No

List three opportunities you currently have in pursuit of your dreams:

1. _____

_____

2. _____

_____

3. _____

_____

"Choose to have the proper mindset when working on growth."

-Chip Baker

Strive to be mentally tough. It is tough to get through tough things. The tough things make you tough. Tough people do tough things. Be Mentally Tough! It's a great path!

We become mentally tough by understanding three things. The first is if you limit yourself, you limit yourself. Second, the possibilities are possible. Third, opportunities bring opportunities. Mindset is developed by understanding limits, possibilities, and opportunities.

ABOUT THE AUTHOR:

Social Media:

IG @chipbakertsc

FB @chipbakertsc

LinkedIn: @chipbakerthesuccesschronicles

Email chipbakertsc@gmail.com

Chip Baker is a fourth-generation educator. He has been a teacher/coach for over twenty-three years. He is a multiple-time best-selling Author, Youtuber/Podcaster, Motivational Speaker and Life Coach.

Chip Baker is the creator of the YouTube channel/podcast "Chip Baker - The Success Chronicles" where he interviews people from all walks of life and shares their stories for positive inspiration and motivation.

Live. Learn. Serve. Inspire. Go get it!

Chip Baker Books

Growing Through Your Go Through

Effective Conversation to Ignite Relationships

Suited For Success Vol. 2

The Formula Chart for Life

The Impact of Influence

R.O.C.K. Solid

The Impact of Influence Vol. 2

Kids Book- Stay On The Right P.A.T.H.

The Impact of Influence Vol. 3

Black Men Love

The Impact of Influence Vol. 4

EYES ON THE HEART

Darryl W. Thomas, Jr.

Have you ever experienced a life changing moment where you had to make an immediate decision?

- o Yes
- o No

Describe that experience:

_____

_____

_____

_____

_____

Did that moment have a positive or negative impact on your life?

- o Positive
- o Negative

Explain the impact of that moment on your life:

_____

_____

_____

_____

_____

_____

How did your decision impact others?

_____

_____

_____

_____

_____

Without knowing the vision, you will find yourself:

- **Fighting fights that are not worth fighting.**
- **Exerting unnecessary energy.**
- **Wasting valuable resources to include time, talent, and treasures.**

Do you have a vision for your life?

o   Yes

o   No

Give a brief description of your vision:

_____

_____

_____

_____

_____

What talents are you using to pursue your vision each day?

_____

_____

_____

_____

_____

Does your vision intimidate you?

- o   Yes
- o   No

Have you ever stopped pursuing your vision due to fear?

- o   Yes
- o   No

What are your fears when thinking about your vision?

_____

_____

_____

_____

_____

_____

_____

_____

_____

_____

_____

_____

_____

_____

_____

List five people in your life that can help you in the areas that intimidate you:

1. _____
2. _____
3. _____
4. _____
5. _____

In what area(s) can the first person listed help you?

_____

_____

_____

_____

_____

In what area(s) can the second person listed help you?

_____

_____

_____

_____

_____

In what area(s) can the third person listed help you?

_____

_____

_____

_____

_____

In what area(s) can the fourth person listed help you?

_____

_____

_____

_____

_____

In what area(s) can the fifth person listed help you?

_____

_____

_____

_____

_____

> **Character is the essence of a person. It is who they are authentically. Leadership is the ability to influence others.**

Survey the 5 people closest to you and ask them how they would define your character:

1. _____
   _____
   _____

2. _____
   _____
   _____

3. _____
   _____
   _____

4. _____
   _____
   _____

5. _____
   _____
   _____

Do you keep the promises you make to others?

- o   Yes
- o   No

Do you keep the promises you make to yourself?

- o   Yes
- o   No

List the top promises you made to others that you need to fulfill:

_____

_____

_____

_____

_____

_____

_____

_____

_____

_____

_____

List the top promises you made to yourself that you need to fulfill:

_____

_____

_____

_____

_____

_____

_____

_____

_____

_____

_____

Do you feel like you fit in with those around you?

- o Yes
- o No

Do you feel like you seek the approval of others?

- o Yes
- o No

Are the people in your circle helping you get closer to your vision?

- o Yes
- o No

On a scale of 1 to 10 how much effort do you give in pursuit of your vision?

_____

What are the areas you need to increase your effort?

_____
_____
_____
_____
_____
_____
_____
_____

> **When you know that you are destined for greatness and are uniquely created to leave a peculiar mark on this world, you move, act, and think differently.**

What characteristics or talents separates you from others?

_____
_____
_____
_____
_____
_____
_____
_____
_____
_____
_____
_____
_____
_____
_____

Are there any dreams you have left unfulfilled?

- o Yes
- o No

Do you see yourself as successful?

- o Yes
- o No

> **Anyone who desires to win and is committed to the process can look up one day and realize that they are a success story. But it cannot and will not happen aside from work.**

Write your personal success story:

_____

_____

_____

_____

_____

_____

_____

_____

_____

_____

_____

_____

_____

_____

_____

_____

_____

_____

_____

_____

_____

The key to winning is more than having a desire to win.

The key is to become a winner.

Keep your eyes on your heart.

Identify how you perceive yourself.

Authentically be who you say you are.

Persistently monitor the motives of your heart.

Then you will become who you were created to be – a winning you.

ABOUT THE AUTHOR:

Social Media:

IG @1darrylwthomas

FB @1darrylwthomas

LinkedIn: @1darrylwthomas

Email darrylwthomasjr@gmail.com

Darryl W. Thomas, Jr. is a U.S. Marine Corps Veteran with more than 20 years of experience helping young adults transform trauma into triumph. Darry is a certified Life Coach and Master Communicator, and the CEO and Senior At-Risk Interventionist of Committed 2 Win, LLC (a personal and leadership development company).

Darryl is a former at-risk student who witness the tragic passing of his father as a high school freshman and endured the abandonment of his mother suffered from drug abuse. Not only has Darryl defied all odds, but he has also made it his life's purpose to coach leadership and character education to underserved youth in secondary and post-secondary education.

He has gone from training military troops to coaching leadership and character to the next generation of leaders in post-secondary education. Darryl's empowering message and communication style resonates with diverse groups of first generation, low-income & disabled college students including Baylor University, McLennan Community College, Faith & Sports Institute (FSI), HBCU Rising Mentors, Advancement Via Individual Determination (AVID) plus more.

Darryl is a 3x Amazon Best-Selling Author as well as an International Best-Selling Author. His most notable publishing is his personal memoir entitled, TODAY... I WIN: When Tests Go Beyond The Classroom.

He and his phenomenal wife believe whole-heartedly that a candle loses nothing by lighting another candle. His primary focus in life is to impact generational transformation.

Darryl's personal mission is to help transform 1 million young people into leaders of change starting with his five children and the young kings and queens that he and his team mentor at the The Size Of a Man – 501(c)3 organization dedicated to breaking the cycles of fatherlessness and poverty. Simply put, Darryl is convinced that a person is purposed to win as long as they don't quit.

SERVICES OFFERED AT COMMITTED 2 WIN

Student Conferences & Workshops

Leadership Camps

Reading Literacy Programs

Educational Consultation

Staff Development Workshops

Leadership & Character Development Programs (school based & SEL curriculum)

Keynote Presentations (commencements, convocations, student assemblies, etc.)

KEYNOTE TOPICS INCLUDE:

GRIT: The Art of Being Faithful to Your Commitment

Suicide Prevention

Leveraging Your Imagination for Success

Winning on Purpose

No More Distractions & Insecurities: Eliminating the Noise

Mastering the Way You Talk

LOVE IS WINNING

Derrick Pearson

Are you competitive?

- o Yes
- o No

Are you a go-to person in clutch situations?

- o Yes
- o No

Describe the feelings you experience when big moments occur in your life:

_____

_____

_____

_____

_____

_____

_____

_____

_____

_____

_____

_____

_____

> **A winning mindset requires that we determine what winning is, and then what is required for it to happen.**

Write a brief explanation of what winning means to you:

_____

_____

_____

_____

_____

_____

_____

_____

_____

_____

What is your routine to prepare for major moments in your life?

_____

_____

_____

_____

_____

_____

_____

_____

_____

_____

_____

Are you satisfied when you achieve your goals?

- o Yes
- o No

Describe a time that you didn't achieve a goal you went after:

_____

_____

_____

_____

_____

_____

_____

_____

_____

_____

What lessons did you learn as a result?

_____

_____

_____

_____

_____

_____

_____

_____

_____

_____

_____

_____

_____

_____

_____

_____

_____

"Win or learn. Never lose."

Do you celebrate the talents you already have?

- o   Yes
- o   No

What are your top 3 talents?

1. _____
2. _____
3. _____

What do you do to strengthen the first talent listed?

_____

_____

_____

What do you do to strengthen the second talent listed?

_____

_____

_____

What do you do to strengthen the third talent listed?

_____

_____

_____

> **Love first, love last, and in between...LOVE MORE.**

When working with others do you establish boundaries?

- o Yes
- o No

What are some boundaries that feel are necessary for a successful project?

_____
_____
_____
_____
_____
_____
_____
_____
_____
_____
_____
_____
_____
_____

Do you set clear expectations to ensure success for each project?

- o Yes
- o No

How do you respond when people do not respect the boundaries of the project?

_____

_____

_____

_____

_____

Do you feel comfortable setting boundaries?

- o Yes
- o No

How do you respond when a project does not meet your expectations?

_____

_____

_____

_____

_____

Are you comfortable making adjustments once a plan is set in motion?

- o Yes
- o No

Describe a time that you had to change your plan to meet the goal:

_____

_____

_____

_____

_____

_____

_____

_____

_____

Winning is relative.

The details required are important.

What kind of team, talent, and heart does your team have?

What kind of team, talent, and heart is the end goal?

ABOUT THE AUTHOR:

Social Media:

IG @derrickpearson

FB @derrick.pearson.5

LinkedIn: @derrick-pearson-b5580524

Email pearsonderrick@aol.com

Derrick Pearson- Sports Radio Station Owner KNTK-FM Lincoln, Nebraska. Co-Host "Old School with Jay Foreman" "DP One on One" at 93.7 The Ticket FM Lincoln, Nebraska. Speaker-TEDxLander May 2019. The love Project Speaker-TEDxDeerPark March 2020. An American Face 3X Amazon Best Selling Author "The Impact of Influence, (Volumes 1,2, 4) Rebuilt Through Recovery

Derrick "DP" Pearson DP has spent stops during his career as a sportscaster, radio and television host, writer, manager and high school coach. That career has taken him nationwide, including Washington, DC, Charlotte, Los Angeles, Salt Lake City, and Atlanta. In addition to his media and coaching ventures, he also helped establish Fat Guy Charities in Charlotte, an NFL Charity, and developed LovePrints, a national mentor program that promotes Loving and Learning through Sports. DP joins Jay Foreman every weekday from 8:00 am – 10:00 am. One on One with DP airs weekdays from 10:00 – 11:00 each weekday morning.

SUCCESS MEANS SACRIFICE

Deuce Malone

What is your ideal career?

_____

_____

_____

_____

_____

What do you do to study the field each week?

_____

_____

_____

_____

_____

_____

_____

_____

Name the top 5 industry leaders in this field?

1. _____

2. _____

3. _____

4. _____

5. _____

Have you attempted to contact any of the leaders in your field?

- o Yes
- o No

What is the contact information for the first person listed above?

Name _____

Company _____

Email Address _____

Phone Number _____

What is the contact information for the second person listed above?

Name _____

Company _____

Email Address _____

Phone Number _____

What is the contact information for the third person listed above?

Name _____

Company _____

Email Address _____

Phone Number _____

What is the contact information for the fourth person listed above?

Name _____

Company _____

Email Address _____

Phone Number _____

What is the contact information for the fifth person listed above?

Name _____

Company _____

Email Address _____

Phone Number _____

> **When you dig into your passion, people will begin to notice, because it emanates from you.**

Do people look to you for information in your ideal career?

- o   Yes
- o   No

How much time do you dedicate each week to studying your ideal career?

- o   0 - 5 hours
- o   5 - 10 hours
- o   10 – 20 hours
- o   20 hours or more

Have you found a mentor or coach in your ideal career?

- o   Yes
- o   No

What are you willing to sacrifice to get into your ideal career?

_____

_____

_____

_____

_____

_____

_____

_____

_____

> **On the way to success, it takes a lot of long nights with no payoff. A lot of long days with minimal to no profit. You need to have a winning mindset and understand that the sacrifices you make today, will pay off tomorrow.**

List 10 upcoming events in your career field that you will attend in the next 12 months:

1. _____
2. _____
3. _____
4. _____
5. _____
6. _____
7. _____
8. _____
9. _____
10. _____

What types of people will you attempt to connect with at those events?

_____
_____
_____
_____
_____
_____
_____
_____
_____
_____
_____

What value will you add to the people that you meet in your career field?

_____

_____

_____

_____

_____

_____

_____

_____

_____

Would you take the opportunity work in a lower position if it would help you get to your ideal career field?

- o   Yes
- o   No

When you aim to get 1% better at your passion every day and surround yourself with like-minded individuals working toward the same goal, you will achieve what you want.

The funny thing is, it may not 100% materialize the way you envisioned it, but you will get there.

ABOUT THE AUTHOR:

Social Media:

IG @theworldofdeuce

FB @theworldofdeuce

LinkedIn: @deucemalone

Email deuce@theworldofdeuce.com

Deuce Malone is a twenty-year music industry vet with experience in retail, FM radio, artist management, festival organization, deejaying, and as an artist. Currently, Deuce serves as President of Wiz Up Entertainment, home of GRAMMY award-winning producer TROY NōKA he is also the CEO of Hustle My Religion apparel, and a member of the Recording Academy of America. In his spare time, Deuce is an avid gamer and sneakerhead with over 150 sneakers in his personal collection.

He is also a huge sports fan. He supports all teams from his hometown in the Houston area –especially the Houston Rockets. You can also find him at most University of Texas Longhorn football and basketball games.

Deuce lives by the phrase, "Emotions will leave you broke."

Broke—as in emotionally hurt, and broke—as in penniless. He strives to act with integrity and temper emotions at all times. Bringing a smile to others' faces is what makes him happy. You can find Deuce online on all social media platforms under @TheWorldOfDeuce and in the live music capital of the world, Austin, TX.

MENTAL ROOTS

Ereka Howard

Are you afraid to fail?

- o Yes

- o No

What emotions come to mind when you think about failure?

_____

_____

_____

_____

_____

_____

_____

_____

_____

Have you ever dealt with depression?

- o Yes

- o No

Have you or anyone in your family ever been diagnosed with a mental illness?

- o Yes

- o No

> **Depression can come from the following areas:**
> - **Genetics - One of the most influential factors in the onset of major depression is based on your genetic code.**
> - **Substance Abuse - early childhood experiences or even major life events (Both Immediate and Prolonged).**

Have you ever dealt with alcohol or substance abuse?

- o Yes
- o No

How do you deal with failure in your life?

_____
_____
_____
_____
_____
_____
_____

What lessons have you learned from those perceived failures?

_____
_____
_____
_____
_____
_____
_____
_____
_____
_____

> **To have a winning mindset, you must be ok with failure. True determination is a result of persevering further than those who gave up in life.**

Are you willing to persist until you succeed?

- o Yes
- o No

How do you restructure your personal thoughts and feelings after a perceived failure?

_____
_____
_____
_____
_____
_____
_____
_____
_____
_____

How do you reward yourself after you accomplish a personal goal?

_____
_____
_____
_____
_____
_____
_____

THE CYCLE OF THOUGHTS AND BEHAVIORS

- Inaccurate, negative perceptions, or thoughts contribute to emotional distress and mental health concerns.

- These thoughts sometimes lead to unhelpful or harmful behaviors.

- Eventually, these thoughts and resulting behaviors can become a pattern that repeats itself.

- Learning how to address and change these patterns can help you deal with problems as they arise, which can help reduce future distress.

ABOUT THE AUTHOR:

Social Media:

IG @msmotivational

FB @erekahowardmotivationalspeaker

LinkedIn: @mserekahoward

Email mserekahoward@gmail.com

Ms. Ereka Howard is no one-dimensional sensation.

She is a speaker, co-author, Certified Life Coach, Clinician, and Adoptee. Since the precocious age of eight, Ms. Ereka Howard has graced and impacted audiences throughout the nation alongside her adoptive mother. Ms. Ereka Howard has been recognized as an authority on motivation, peak performance, and peer leadership which has made her well respected amongst her community and audience. Ms. Ereka Howard creates an authentic connection with her audience as they think, laugh, applaud and remain engaged. Due to her ability to relate to and transform people's lives, she is a highly regarded nationally sought-after speaker. Ms. Ereka Howard displays knowledge, wisdom, and engaging speaking styles riddled with humor and captivating stories which have made her an asset to partnerships and audiences. After overcoming many hurdles throughout her life, Ms. Ereka Howard now shares her life experiences and teaches the community how to be successful throughout life. Ms. Ereka Howard has dedicated her life to the empowerment of everyone. She is a fresh voice for a new generation. Ms. Ereka Howard has a Bachelor of Science in Exercise and Sports Science and a Master in Clinical Mental Health Counseling. Ereka is currently working on a Doctorate in Counseling Education and Supervision.

WHAT IS THE REAL SECRET TO WINNING?

Hoss Tabrizi

> **The Four Keys to a Winning Mindset**
>
> - **Have a goal in mind**
> - **Be resilient**
> - **Work hard until you achieve your goal**
> - **Learn and grow.**

Do you strive to outwork others?

- ○ Yes
- ○ No

Do you walk into your opportunities knowing that you will be victorious?

- ○ Yes
- ○ No

Are you confident in your abilities?

- ○ Yes
- ○ No

> **You have the ability to change a negative to a positive quickly. Or treat a loss as a lesson instead of defeat.**

What is daily work regimen in pursuit of your goals?

_____
_____
_____
_____
_____
_____
_____
_____
_____
_____

Do you strive to outwork others?

- o Yes
- o No

How do you define success?

_____
_____
_____
_____
_____
_____
_____

In your opinion, which of the following makes you a winner?

- o Raising a child
- o Being better than yesterday
- o Being a doctor or lawyer
- o Having 10 million dollars in net worth
- o Having a relationship with God
- o Donating regularly
- o Owning a Jet
- o Protecting others from bullies
- o Having a multi-million-dollar home
- o Owning an expensive car
- o Serving your country
- o Saving someone's life
- o Leading with love

Do you see failure as an opportunity to reset and start over?

- o Yes
- o No

Are you able to help others see the best in themselves?

- o Yes
- o No

Name 5 people in your life that you can help reframe the way they see themselves:

1. _____
2. _____
3. _____
4. _____
5. _____

What will you do to help the first person you listed reframe the way they see themselves?

_____
_____
_____
_____
_____

What will you do to help the second person you listed reframe the way they see themselves?

_____
_____
_____
_____
_____

What will you do to help the third person you listed reframe the way they see themselves?

_____
_____
_____
_____
_____

What will you do to help the fourth person you listed reframe the way they see themselves?

_____
_____
_____
_____
_____

What will you do to help the fifth person you listed reframe the way they see themselves?

_____

_____

_____

_____

_____

Take your winning mindset and
put that energy towards
something you desire.

Be determined with your actions.

Win the day.

Win the week.

Win the month.

Win the year.

Win!

ABOUT THE AUTHOR:

Social Media:

IG @hosstabrizi

FB @hoss.tabrizi

LinkedIn: @hosstabrizi

Email hoss.tabrizi@nm.com

Hoss Tabrizi is the son of Mehdi and Nahid and brother to Nahaleh. He's married to Carolyn, and together they have three children: Maximus, Mia, and Michael. He's a financial advisor, coach, bestselling author, public speaker, and community leader.

Hoss genuinely wants to help people become better and to discover their inner greatness. He cares about seeing improvement in himself and in those that he interacts with. Hoss communicates with people in a way that motivates them to have confidence and conviction on their journey towards self-improvement in their personal, professional, and financial lives. Just like his father, he wants to leave this world better than he found it.

DREAM, DARE, & DISCIPLINE

Kenneth Wilson

Do you visualize yourself winning?

- o   Yes
- o   No

When you visualize yourself winning do you include the potential obstacles?

- o   Yes
- o   No

Can you imagine the winning celebration in your honor?

- o   Yes
- o   No

Describe the feelings you will have when you achieve your goal:

_____

_____

_____

_____

_____

_____

_____

_____

_____

Imagine that you have achieved your ultimate goal. Write an acceptance speech in the lines below:

_____

_____

_____

_____

_____

_____

_____

_____

_____

_____

_____

_____

_____

_____

_____

_____

_____

_____

_____

_____

_____

_____

_____

_____

_____

_____

_____

_____

_____

Who is someone that you look up to on your journey?

_____

_____

What were some of the obstacles they had to overcome to achieve their goals?

_____

_____

_____

_____

_____

_____

_____

_____

What have you learned from their journey?

_____

_____

_____

_____

What can you implement in your life based on their journey?

_____

_____

_____

_____

_____

_____

_____

_____

Three basic principles:

DREAM
DARE
DISCIPLINE

Visualize your journey from start to finish. Describe the journey in detail below:

_____
_____
_____
_____
_____
_____
_____
_____
_____
_____
_____
_____
_____
_____
_____
_____
_____
_____
_____
_____
_____
_____

Do you have a daily routine?

- o Yes
- o No

What activities do you do each day in pursuit of your dreams?

_____

_____

_____

_____

_____

_____

_____

Write out your daily schedule below:

- ▪ 5am _____
- ▪ 6am _____
- ▪ 7am _____
- ▪ 8am _____
- ▪ 9am _____
- ▪ 10am _____
- ▪ 11am _____
- ▪ 12pm _____
- ▪ 1pm _____
- ▪ 2pm _____
- ▪ 3pm _____
- ▪ 4pm _____
- ▪ 5pm _____
- ▪ 6pm _____
- ▪ 7pm _____
- ▪ 8pm _____
- ▪ 9pm _____
- ▪ 10pm _____

> **You cannot be afraid to act on your dreams. You may be afraid to fail, but you'll never know if you don't try. To dare, you need motivation and determination from the dream.**

What is your biggest fear on the path to your success?

_____

_____

_____

_____

_____

What is your biggest area of opportunity?

_____

_____

_____

_____

_____

What do you do to improve upon your weaknesses?

_____

_____

_____

_____

_____

> **Discipline is the rules, conduct, and boundaries we live by. It helps us stay focused and gives us the fortitude we need to stay on track.**

Do you have enough discipline to become successful?

- o Yes
- o No

Do you have a system in place that keeps you focused?

- o Yes
- o No

If not, why?

_____

_____

_____

If yes, explain your system:

_____

_____

_____

_____

_____

_____

_____

_____

_____

_____

Life and entrepreneurship have
many challenges. Possessing a
winning mindset can make the
journey a little easier.

Continue to dream

Dare to keep going

Have discipline to see it through!

ABOUT THE AUTHOR:

Social Media:

IG @mrkennethwilson

FB @mrkennethwilson

LinkedIn: @kennywilson65

Email kennywilson65@gmail.com

Kenneth Wilson is a native of Silver Spring, MD. He is the Founder and CEO of Men of Stature and Black Squirrel Media. He has professional experience in business, education, politics, and public safety. He is also a passionate community advocate who has worked with people globally.

As a consultant, he has worked with businesses, non-profit organizations, churches, and political outfits all over the world. He has developed programs that have helped dozens of aspiring entrepreneurs begin and pursue their business dreams.

He also has a passion to be a voice in the community, which includes hosting several podcasts and virtual shows. Kenneth can be heard weekly as Co-Host of the Community Coalition Show, Reason & Rhyme Podcast, and The Speakeasy Show.

As a public speaker, he discusses issues involving the Black community, with a focus on Black men. He also discusses and teaches seminars on business development. In the field of safety, he is a certified CPR/First Aid Instructor. He teaches courses in person and virtually.

Accomplishments
- 2016 President's Lifetime Achievement Award Winner
- Two-time Bestselling Author
- Founder and CEO of Black Squirrel Media & Men of Stature
- Creator of the B.LIT Festival & Black Squirrel Media Network

International Safety Expert and Community Advocate

MENTAL HEALTH AND THE WINNING MINDSET

Kristen Davis

What do you focus on throughout the day?

_____

_____

_____

_____

_____

Do you focus on winning daily?

- o Yes
- o No

Have you tapped into the power of positive thinking?

- o Yes
- o No

Do you feel like you deserve to be successful?

- o Yes
- o No

Are you afraid of success?

- o Yes
- o No

> **If you fix your mind on succeeding, the behaviors needed for that success are likely to follow and success will be more likely. The more we think about things, the more likely we are to try to make those things a reality.**

How much of your success do you attribute to luck?

_____

Have traumatic experiences from your past created a mental block for your success?

- o   Yes
- o   No

Describe the most traumatic experience in your own words:

_____
_____
_____
_____
_____
_____
_____
_____
_____
_____
_____
_____
_____
_____
_____
_____

> **Unresolved issues will try to convince you that you cannot be successful and that you do not deserve the things you want. Past traumas and hurt can block out the idea that you can have a good life and win.**

Write a brief letter to your younger self about the traumatic experience. Explain how the experience has affected you in your current life:

_____

_____

_____

_____

_____

_____

_____

_____

_____

_____

_____

_____

_____

_____

_____

_____

_____

_____

_____

_____

_____

Create a list of things that you feel you deserve in life at this moment:

_____

_____

_____

_____

_____

_____

_____

_____

What are the self-sabotaging beliefs that you feel are keeping you from the things you listed above?

_____

_____

_____

_____

Create a list of beliefs that you can use to replace those self-sabotaging beliefs above:

_____

_____

_____

_____

_____

_____

_____

_____

_____

_____

_____

> **Instead of thinking about the unpleasant things that you experienced as something that happened to you, try to rephrase the event as something that empowered or taught you.**

Do you practice daily affirmations?

- o Yes
- o No

Write a list of 10 affirmations that you can repeat daily:

1. _____
2. _____
3. _____
4. _____
5. _____
6. _____
7. _____
8. _____
9. _____
10. _____

What do you do for your personal self-care?

_____
_____
_____
_____
_____
_____
_____
_____

What do you do to take care of your personal health?

_____

_____

_____

_____

_____

Do you exercise regularly?

- o Yes
- o No

How would you define your eating habits?

- o Healthy
- o Needs work
- o Couch-potato

How much time do you take in the following each day?

- o News
- o Radio
- o Music
- o Podcasts
- o Books
- o Magazines
- o Social Media

To achieve a winning mindset, you must focus on your mental health.

First, you must make sure that you have addressed negative emotions and past hang ups. This will free you to begin pursuing that next level.

Next, you should focus on taking care of yourself, which allows your mental health to be at its best. You must also take this time to monitor what you are taking in, making sure that most of the time is spent being productive and moving towards your goal, while making sure to take breaks to stay balanced.

By doing these things, you increase your mental wellness and can use your winning mindset to achieve your goals.

ABOUT THE AUTHOR:

Social Media:

IG @kristendavislpc

FB @kristendavislpc

LinkedIn: @kristendavislpc

Email kristen.gtrc@gmail.com

Kristen Davis is a Licensed Professional Therapist with years of experience in private practice. During her time as a therapist, she has worked in the areas of substance abuse and addiction, trauma, depression, anxiety, life planning, Transition, Neurodivergent populations and Career Readiness. Additionally, Kristen works as a Regional Transition Program Specialist for the Gulf Coast Region of Texas Workforce Solutions - Vocational Rehabilitation Services, implementing programming for students with disabilities and providing feedback on effectiveness to Regional and State administration.

She has a personal tie to Trauma, PTSD, and Depression after her brother was murdered. Although it was a horrible experience, this has helped Kristen to expand her knowledge on grief and overcoming substantial mental stress and strain. This experience was so transformative, that it moved her to write a book detailing her battle with grief and how to utilize therapeutic practices in real life and speak to audiences.

Kristen has a Bachelor of Arts in Psychology and Master of Science in Mental Health/Rehabilitation from Mississippi State University.

I FOUND MY LIGHT WHEN YOU LEFT ME IN THE DARK

Monica Earl Washington

> **You need God and confidence to make things happen powerfully within your life. To build and establish a winning mindset, you will need to have a strong effective prayer life which includes fasting and meditation in a higher God.**

Are you confident in yourself?

- o Yes
- o No

Do you have a prayer life?

- o Yes
- o No

What are some things you pray about in your personal life?

_____

_____

_____

_____

_____

Have you ever done a spiritual fast?

- o Yes
- o No

If no, are you open to learning more about spiritual fasting?

- o Yes
- o No

If yes, describe the experience below:

_____

_____

_____

_____

_____

_____

_____

_____

_____

_____

Who is in your support circle?

_____

_____

_____

_____

_____

List 5 lessons you learned as a child that you have had to retrain yourself about:

1. _____
2. _____
3. _____
4. _____
5. _____

What was the new lesson for the first lesson listed above?

_____

_____

_____

_____

_____

What was the new lesson for the second lesson listed above?

_____

_____

_____

_____

_____

What was the new lesson for the third lesson listed above?

_____

_____

_____

_____

_____

What was the new lesson for the fourth lesson listed above?

_____

_____

_____

_____

_____

What was the new lesson for the fifth lesson listed above?

_____

_____

_____

_____

_____

Have you ever experienced verbal or physical abuse?

- o Yes
- o No

If yes, how has that affected you mentally?

_____

_____

_____

_____

_____

Do you blame yourself for the abuse you experienced?

- o Yes
- o No

In the lines below, write a brief letter empowering your younger self who was abused:

_____

_____

_____

_____

_____

_____

_____

_____

_____

_____

_____

_____

_____

_____

_____

_____

Were there people who attempted to rescue you from the abusive situation?

- o Yes
- o No

In the lines below, write a brief letter thanking those people who attempted to help:

_____

_____

_____

_____

_____

_____

_____

_____

_____

_____

_____

_____

_____

_____

_____

_____

_____

_____

List your 10 favorite inspirational scriptures:

1. _____
2. _____
3. _____
4. _____
5. _____
6. _____
7. _____
8. _____
9. _____
10. _____

How will you apply the first scripture to your own life?

_____
_____
_____
_____
_____

How will you apply the second scripture to your own life?

_____
_____
_____
_____
_____

How will you apply the third scripture to your own life?

_____
_____
_____
_____
_____

How will you apply the fourth scripture to your own life?

_____

_____

_____

_____

_____

How will you apply the fifth scripture to your own life?

_____

_____

_____

_____

_____

How will you apply the sixth scripture to your own life?

_____

_____

_____

_____

_____

How will you apply the seventh scripture to your own life?

_____

_____

_____

_____

_____

How will you apply the eighth scripture to your own life?

_____

_____

_____

_____

_____

How will you apply the ninth scripture to your own life?

_____

_____

_____

_____

_____

How will you apply the tenth scripture to your own life?

_____

_____

_____

_____

_____

Create a list of generational curses you would like to break for your family:

_____

_____

_____

_____

_____

Write down 10 things you would like to have in your life:

1. _____
2. _____
3. _____
4. _____
5. _____
6. _____
7. _____
8. _____
9. _____
10. _____

You can have a better life if you implement the following:

A strong prayer life

Confidence in yourself

Refuse to let others define you through their self-limiting beliefs

A strong work ethic

A personal relationship with God or your higher power

Faith

ABOUT THE AUTHOR:

Social Media:

IG @monicaneecyearlwashington

FB @monicaneecyearlwashington

LinkedIn: @monicaneecyearlwashington

Email neecysoftandsweet@yahoo.com

Ms. Monica Earl Washington, nick name "Neecy," (short for Monica's middle name Denise) was born in Fort Campbell, Kentucky. She was raised in Clarksville, Tennessee, graduating from the legendary Burt Junior High School. She graduated from Northeast High School, Class of 1983. It is at Burt Junior High School where Monica found her passion for writing and learned to keep private dated and organized journals of her daily life.

Monica was the owner of Queenrodney Christian Cleaning Services of Jacksonville, Florida, cleaning million-dollar homes for elite clientele including several NFL football players. Monica is currently the owner of Neecy's Soft and Sweet Holistic Organic Southern Scents. Monica is the mother of two handsome sons, James "Tank" Earl, and Reginald Kilo Banks. She is the Gma of two beautiful angels, Corinthian "Corey" Earl, and Naomi Earl. Monica currently resides in Washington, DC and works for the Washington Headquarters (Pentagon). She loves to meet great people.

Monica famous saying, "Don't watch me, watch God!

AGAINST ALL ODDS

Reggie Rusk

> **You must have a winning mindset to obtain success, or you will live your life building someone else's dreams.**

Do you believe that you deserve to be successful?

- ○ Yes
- ○ No

Do you tend to see the positive or negative in every situation?

- ○ Positive
- ○ Negative

Survey the 5 people closest to you. Do they describe you as having a positive or negative mindset?

Person 1 _____

Person 2 _____

Person 3 _____

Person 4 _____

Person 5 _____

Are you able to find solutions when you are facing difficult situations?

- o Yes
- o No

Do you take time to visualize the success you want in life?

- o Yes
- o No

Write out the vision you have for your future self. Be as descriptive as possible:

_____

_____

_____

_____

_____

_____

_____

_____

_____

_____

_____

_____

_____

_____

_____

_____

_____

_____

_____

_____

> **The beginning stage of having a winning mindset is first having a vision. If you can't see yourself having success, it's virtually impossible to obtain success.**

Are you committed to the process of becoming successful?

- o Yes
- o No

What are you willing to sacrifice to become successful?

_____

_____

_____

_____

_____

What are you unwilling to sacrifice to become successful?

_____

_____

_____

_____

_____

How do you respond to constructive feedback?

_____

_____

_____

_____

_____

_____

> **We must be able to persevere through adverse situations to grow. Perseverance is key to a winning mindset. Everything will not go the way you plan it, so stay focused on the goal no matter what.**

Do you fold under pressure?

- o Yes
- o No

Have you ever dealt with opposition from friends or family?

- o Yes
- o No

How did you deal with it?

_____

_____

_____

_____

_____

How will you deal with it in the future?

_____

_____

_____

_____

_____

_____

_____

_____

_____

Describe a time that you faced an extreme amount of pressure. Explain how you responded below:

_____

_____

_____

_____

_____

_____

_____

_____

_____

How would you respond differently with a Winning Mindset?

_____

_____

_____

_____

_____

_____

_____

_____

_____

_____

_____

_____

_____

_____

_____

_____

_____

_____

You can have a better life if you implement the following:

A strong prayer life

Confidence in yourself

Refuse to let others define you through their self-limiting beliefs

A strong work ethic

A personal relationship with God or your higher power

Faith

ABOUT THE AUTHOR:

Social Media:

IG @coachreggie_

FB @coachreggie25

LinkedIn: @reggierusk

Email reggierusk@gmail.com

Beginning In 1996 Coach Reggie had the opportunity to play in the NFL for 5 seasons and played with 3 teams. Coach Reggie's path to the NFL was not a straight one.

Reggie knows first-hand how difficult it is for a young athlete. He had no offers after his senior year in high school and elected to take the junior college route to continue his education. Reggie's college coaches made a huge impact on him and his success. Growing up in a single parent household, those relationships were invaluable to Reggie's success. After two successful seasons, major D1 colleges were calling. Ultimately, he chose the University of Kentucky and played his final two collegiate seasons there.

Coach Reggie is a former student-athlete and graduate of the University of Kentucky. After watching numerous athletes lose opportunities due to failing grades, low SAT/ACT scores, and lack of recruiting awareness, His mission is to turn dreams into reality by helping student-athletes better prepare themselves physically, academically, and mentally. Play for success has aligned with many athletes, business owners, professionals in the community to create a realistic picture for students of every background.

ABOUT THE LEAD AUTHOR

Sugar Ray is a Motivational Speaker, Author and the CEO of Claim Your Destiny Enterprises, LLC! He has worked with several organizations across the nation to impact the lives of several thousand people! He speaks with organizations about overcoming obstacles in life, improving performance, increasing self-confidence and strategies for tapping into their full potential!

His company Claim Your Destiny Enterprises, LLC. focuses on research not theory. Sugar Ray Destin, Jr. is a nationally sought after motivational speaker. He empowers audiences with his message of hope, passion and the unlimited potential each of us possess! Sugar Ray empowers people across the nation with leadership programs, mentoring programs and college preparation conferences!

His publishing community, BOBM Publishing, LLC. had helped several people fulfill their dream of becoming published authors and create additional income streams using a proven system. To date, they have launched over 300 new authors to #1 Amazon Bestselling Author Status.

PICK UP THESE OTHER TITLES BY SUGAR RAY DESTIN, JR.

THE BUSINESS OF BOOKS

The Business of Books is a book designed to help authors become comfortable with the process of writing their first book. It will also take you into the world of marketing, branding and creating additional streams of income as an Authorpreneur.

CLAIM YOUR DESTINY!

Claim Your Destiny is the book that will help you tap into the unlimited potential you possess! If you are ready for your breakthrough this is the book for you! You will be empowered with the stories of average people who have achieved amazing victories! You will be introduced to tools that will help you master yourself and live your dreams! If you are ready, now is the time for you to Claim Your Destiny!

CLAIM YOUR DESTINY! (WORKBOOK)

The Claim Your Destiny Workbook is a perfect complement for the life-changing book! The workbook will take you through questions and activities that will force you to stretch as you tap into the unlimited potential you possess! Working through the workbook is like having the dynamic coaching of Sugar Ray available 24/7!

SUGARCOATED

This is a book of poems and affirmations about the inner and outer beauty of women. It is a celebration of the grace, elegance and phenomenal strength of the women in our lives.

To order your autographed copies visit
www.sugarraydestin.com/books-by-sugar-ray